The Hearns Story

No More Silence The Truth Shall Be Told

Based on a true story by JESSIE HEARNS

**No More Silence &
The Truth Shall Be Told**

The Hearns Story No More Silence & the Truth Shall be Told Copyright (C) 2024 by Mr. Jessie B. Hearns All rights reserve. This book or parts thereof may not be stored in a retrieval system, reproduced in any form, or transmitted in any form by any means.

Mechanical, photocopy, electronic, recording, or otherwise without prior written permission of the author, Mr. Jessie B. Hearns, except as provided by United States of America copyright law.

Unless indicated in footnotes, all scriptures references, and quotation are written from the King James Version of the Bible.

Worldwide Kingdom Publishing
1911 Horger St
Lincoln Park, Michigan 48146
(313) 544-8010

FIRST EDITION

Email: worldwidekingdompublishing@yahoo.com

ISBN: 978-1-934905-27-2

Printed in the United States of America

No More Silence &
The Truth Shall Be Told

DEDICATION

This book in was written in loving memory of my father, the late John Henry Hearns.

This book is dedicated to the late Joe Lucas Jr., and the late Sam Fenton.

I also dedicate this book to those who had the courage to speak out against child abuse, mental abuse, verbal abuse, and physical abuse.

SPECIAL THANKS

Special thanks, to my Lord & Savior Jesus Christ who have kept me strong throughout the years.

**No More Silence &
The Truth Shall Be Told**

TABLE OF CONTENTS

Dedication
Special Thanks
Introduction

PART ONE: TRUTH REVEALED

1) Chapter 1 ... My Daddy:
   John Henry Hearns   page 25

2) Chapter 2... 5830 Helen   page 29

3) Chapter 3... 20277 Avon   page 37

4) Chapter 4... Family Separation   page 44

5) Chapter 5... Reasons Why We Don't Have a Right to Keep Silent   page 51

PART TWO: THE PROCESS OF HEALING

6) Chapter 6... The Beginning of Healing   page 63

7) Chapter 7... Overcoming the Anger   page 66

8) Chapter 8... Understanding my Purpose   page 71

9) Chapter 8.... No More Silence   page 77

No More Silence &
The Truth Shall Be Told

MASTER CHEF JESSIE B HEARNS

I often tried to ignore my pain to support his fame!

INTRODUCTION

Have you ever been falsely accused as a child? Have you ever been severely punished for something you never did? Have you ever been locked in a dark room with no food and water? Well, I have! Unfortunately, I experienced this process of abuse (hell) from the ages 9-16 years old. My name is Jessie, I am 57 years old and I am now a thriving business entrepreneur. I wish that my success was the direct result of a loving, nurturing upbringing. However, nothing is further from the truth! I grew up in a household where one of the male family members became an international famous sports celebrity, a multi-millionaire. For most people that would be a dream household to grow up in; but certainly that is not my story!

My journey as a child was very traumatic, painful, and filled will emotional abuse, verbal abuse, psychological abuse, mental abuse, and physical abuse. Abuse is the mistreatment of person, child, or animal. It means to treat a person, child, or animal with cruelty or violence. Someone who is callously indifferent and enjoys causing pain and suffering to others is a malicious and dangerous individual. Child abuse is deliberate intentional injury and ill treatment to a child who is under 18 years of age. Child abuse can occur in many ways. As I share my experiences, it is my prayer you will feel what I felt: the pain of betrayal, the fear of not being protected, the shame of being a victim, the loneliness of being made to keep the secret, the anger that has been internalized, and the confusion of trusting God!

Furthermore, my abuser who is my brother, because we share the same mother; not that we share the same biological father. My father who is a Hearns allowed my brother to take his name. The earliest memories of my oldest brother boxing career begin when he was around 16 years old. One day, he was looking out the window and saw three other kids from the neighborhood running to the bus stop to get on the bus. They were taking the bus to the gym to box. So the next day, my brother saw the kids again. When the kids returned he asked them where had they been? They said they had left the gym. The next day he asked, "Mom, can I go to the gym?" And she said, "Yes!" He went with the kids with a pair of gym shoes and shorts. They told my brother he needed boxing shorts and boxing shoes. The next day, mom went and bought him a pair boxing shorts and boxing gym shoes. He was waiting for the guys to come down the street. They told him they would be there after they got out of school. So as the guys finished school he met them on the porch, and they caught the bus to the gym. When they arrived at the gym, their trainer was a man named, Tina Hill. He was the three young guy's trainer, Molly, Phil, and Ricky. That day my brother did his workout. However, Tina decided to work with my brother. The next day he asked my brother, "So you think you want to get in the ring?" He responded, "I think I can beat this guy," and he pointed to one of the best guys in the gym. Tina told him, "No, I don't think I want to put you in the ring with him. Let me put you in the ring with a beginner like you." So when Tina put my brother in the ring with the guy, my brother beat the guy. After that my brother wanted to fight someone else. So Tina put him in the ring with another boxer that was a little better than the first guy, and my brother put a whooping on him. The next day, Tina decided to put him in the ring with someone else who was better that the previous two that he fought, and needless to say my brother put a whipping on him. After that he wanted to fight the main guy. Tina allowed him to fight a few others bouts, then put him in the ring with the main guy. My brother kind of put a whipping on him. After that, Tina was really paying to my brother. He said, "Oh this guy is pretty good. I need to go ahead and train him." So Tina decided to train my brother. They trained together for a few months, until tragedy struck.

One day, Tina had the young guys over at his house playing basketball in his backyard. Unfortunately, Tina had a very mean neighbor who would run outside every time the basketball would go into his yard. This neighbor was so evil when the basketball would bounce in his yard, he would put the basketball in his garage, and slam the door. So Tina would have to go to the store and buy new basketball, because his neighbor would not allow them to jump the fence to get the ball. After a couple of days playing basketball the neighbor was enraged. On the third day, they went out to Tina's backyard playing basketball and the ball went over the fence into Tina's neighbor yard. Tina had just purchased a brand new basketball for the guys to play, and he jumped over the fence to get it. Sadly, his neighbor came out of his house with a double barrel shot gun and shot Tina in the chest and killed him boldly in front of everybody! Leaving the young boxers in training devastated. After Tina Hill died Emmanuel Stewart came along and wanted to train my brother and that was the beginning of their boxing relationship.

In summary, my purpose for writing this book is to break the silence of the abuse, pain, trauma, deception, corruption, manipulation, and betrayal, I experienced as a child. Sadly, there are many people bound by the trauma and the abuse of their past. They go through life suffering in silence. It is important to me that the truth is revealed! The bible tells us, the truth shall make us free, and now I am free! This book was not written to hurt anyone in their wrong doings, nor to breakdown my abusers.

It is truth, that I experienced growing up. You may not like my truth, and you may not believe my truth, and you may not understand my truth and that is your prerogative. You may not even care nor agree with my purpose for writing this book. It is my experience and I want someone who have been victimized by abuse to know they do not have to keep silent anymore. They no longer have to suffer inwardly, while suppressing the pain of abuse, and yet protecting their abusers. It is time to expose your abusers and be heal from the shame, pain, and trauma of abuse. I want those readers who have experienced this same pain to be released from the bondage that comes with every demonic act of abuse. Lastly, this book was written to lift others up by showing them that there is a way out of the pain of abuse and the way of deliverance from this kind of pain comes through prayer! Confess your faults one for another, and pray one for another, that ye may be healed. The effectual fervent prayers of a righteous man availeth much, according to James 5:16. It is a very hurtful experience when you confront your abuser and the people who knew the secrets of your abuse and they minimize the abuse they caused you, by saying it wasn't that bad, or you deserve it. No one deserves to be beat until they are bloody, or locked in a room with no door handles, and no food. It is my prayer that this book will help abusers all across the nations to confess, repent, and apologize before they leave this earth.

**An Awesome Boxing Trainer
the late Tina Hill
He had over 15 boxers who he was
training, when he acquired
"The Hit Man!"**

Boxing Trainer
The late Tina Hill

No More Silence &
The Truth Shall Be Told

The late great Boxing Trainer Emmanuel Stewart

These hands that brought so much fame, and yet they inflicted so much physical pain on me! At that time his hands were registered as a lethal weapon, and they still are....

Many did not know you were a public success, but a wolf in sheep clothing!

PART ONE
TRUTH REVEALED

**God said, "Touch not mine anointed and do my prophets no harm!"
I Chronicles 12:22
TH**

CHAPTER ONE
MY DADDY:
JOHN HENRY HEARNS

This chapter is dedicated to my father, John Henry Hearns, who passed away at age 41, from a massive heart attack in 1980. He was a very firm man, but a fair man. My father met my mom while she was working at a convenience store in Tennessee. My daddy was a truck driver at the time, so he stopped into the store she worked at and delivered some products. There he met my mom and they begin to date. My mom already had three children when they met, but my father vowed to take care of those three as his own. Soon after that they married in the living room of my grandmother's home in Byhalia, Mississippi. After a year of marriage my father's cousin, Johnny Wilkins "Cousin Johnny", convinced my daddy to relocate the family to Detroit, Michigan; because he had a job working at General Motors, and he want my father to work at General Motors, as well. In those days, jobs were plentiful in the automotive industry. So my father moved the family to Detroit, Michigan. When they arrived in Detroit, he decided to apply for a job at the Detroit Police Department, and he was hired. In those days, Black police officers had to walk the beat. They were not allowed to ride in the police cars. Once the Black police officer caught a person committing a crime, he had to call for backup from his Caucasian fellow police officers. They would come, make the arrest, and transport the suspect back to the police department. Then the Black police officers had to walk the beat back to the precinct to complete the paperwork on the arrest.

My parents moved on Griggs street and they start having children, Billy, Sara, John (R.I.P.), Louise, Henry, and myself Jessie Hearns. After a few years, my mom and dad separated and my dad moved back to Memphis, Tennessee. Even though they were separated my dad was still instrumental in the discipline of the children through telephone calls. We still respected him and obeyed his instructions.

Then my mom met a man named, Joe Lucas who moved in and became our stepfather, even though my parents never divorced. This is where the interesting story of No More Silence begins…..

**Mr. John Henry Hearns
(My Father)**

At the Grave site of My Father's Funeral

CHAPTER TWO
MEMORIES of 5830 HELEN

Where do I begin? I am the youngest of nine children. As far back as I can recall I have been abused and my childhood was nothing less than a horror story. Let me explain!

My earliest memories of Helen street begins with me waking up on an unforgettable snowy winter Christmas morning. We were kinda or somewhat poor back then, and we all were given "Goodfella boxes." These boxes were given to families who needed help blessing their children at Christmas and everyone in the family had a box. Inside the boxes were candy, underwear, a pair of pants, and a couple of pair of shoes, which made us extremely excited! Even though, the boxes were under the Christmas tree late, it was still sufficient, because our mother and step-father did not have so much to give out. That Christmas day I remember vividly, because of the beautiful Christmas spirit that permeated throughout the atmosphere of the house. There was the smelling of the food, lots of cooking, eating, and the opening of the gifts. Unfortunately later on that Christmas night, my memory was tarnished by the verbal, mental, emotional, and physical abuse. The cycle of abuse was a continuous every day situation, and it did not even stop for the celebration of Christmas. There hardly ever was any peace in our house; because my mom's method of raising us was to allow the older children to discipline the younger children, which was totally wrong! It was inappropriate, incorrect, and unlawful; because it puts the older children into parental authority while they are yet siblings to the children they are disciplining. Especially, when older brothers and sisters method of discipling become abusive. At that time, I still did not know it was wrong; until one day, I was talking to the neighbor and she began to share knowledge on roles in life. She revealed that kids should not be able to discipline other kids, but this is how some families did it back in the day. This same neighbor also invited me to dinner; where I was waiting to eat, because I was told parents (no matter the circumstances) always ate first. She boldly disagreed! Through her, I learned that children should always be fed before adults. Wow, I was totally shocked! Unfortunately, in my family's household this was not the common practice. It is a sad situation when parents do not consider their children as a high priority. Some parents even ignore their parental responsibilities, and fail to follow through on their duties as parents. Parents have the responsibility of loving, feeding, protecting, providing, teaching, and nurturing their children. When parents repeatedly fail to fulfill their responsibilities to care for their children it becomes neglect, abandonment, and abuse. Know assuredly, anytime children have been neglected, abandoned, and abused they will need mental, and spiritual counseling.

I had a stepfather named "Joe." Joe was basically the banker of the family. He would take us fishing and take us out to Belle Isle. Joe owned a Cadillac, and he would take us out to a good time away from home. Joe was being mentally challenged in this family warfare of dysfunctional relational abuse. He too was deceived and abused because he thought my mom was being faithful to him, in all actuality she was not faithful. She had another man, name "Slim" who is deceased but she met in church. She would lie and tell my stepfather Joe, that Slim worked for the welfare agency. Therefore, every time Slim came over to our house, my stepfather Joe would have to take his plate off the table and go downstairs into the basement to eat to hide from Slim. This game of deception and folly continued for a little over a year or two until truth was revealed. It was an unforgettable joke, one of the neighbors happened to recognized Slim, because he knew him. One day this neighbor asked Joe, "Why is Slim always at your house?" Joe responded, "Oh, he works for the welfare department," and back then a woman could not have a man living in her house if she was on welfare. Joe was told Slim worked for the welfare department, only to be bound by emotional abuse, manipulation and deception. Finally, our neighbor told Joe the truth that Slim was a singer, a gospel singer at Church and that he does not work for the welfare office. Needless to say, Joe was furious and he purposed in his heart to get revenge. One particular night Slim came over and picked up my mom and they when out on a date. When they returned my stepfather Joe, hid behind the door and tried to hit my mother in the head with a hammer, because he realized he was being deceived and Slim did not work at the welfare office. As a result, my family began to fight and my stepfather had a prosthetic leg when he fell, my oldest brother came and took his leg off. Joe could not walk at this point and then they kinda beat him up, so he could not walk or move. There were many incidents that happened after Joe and my mother had the fight. As I reflect, I remember everyone was outside playing and I came in the house to get some water and smelled smoke. Immediately, I told my mother that I smelled smoke coming from upstairs so when she went upstairs following the smoke, she realized the closet was on fire. Instantly, she called for other family members to help her put out the fire and eradicate the smoke. When they finally put the fire out, I was falsely accused for setting the

fire. I pleaded and tried to explain my case repeatedly to no avail! When I was taken upstairs and made to lay down, I was wrapped in three sheets mimicking a straight jacket with my hand to my side where my hands was down to my sides and rolled up in the sheets and laid on the bed, my mom, Tommy, and Mary laid me down face up and put matches in between my toes. They put five matches in between each toes. Therefore, as one was lit, the others lit up consecutively, all I could do was just lay there and scream, "It wasn't me!" I could not reach my toes because my hands was wrapped along by my sides in three layers of sheets! All I could hear was them laughing, this should teach you a lesson. I bet you won't set nothing else on fire! I was tormented by these words of mockery repeatedly throughout my life, and even to this present day I still can hear those words in my
mind.

Another incident at this house, with nine siblings food was very scarce. My brother and I took a ham from out of the refrigerator. We carried the ham upstairs and ate it, because we were very hungry. Needless to say, we were caught and we both received a whipping. My punishment was also being locked in a room upstairs with the door knobs taking off. With me knowing that could be part of my punishment, I previously took screwdrivers and spoons into the room so I could jimmy the door and get out! As a result, being locked in the room was also a part of my punishment for eating the ham. I did get out of the room and I was caught. That's when the abuse became worst. They wrapped me around a pole in the basement, in sheets like a mummy. Then they took an extension cord and tied it around the sheets to make sure I would not be able to get out. They turned off the lights, and it was pitch black (I couldn't see anything). Suddenly, a pregnant roach crawled all over my face and eventually went into my ear, and got stuck in my ear. It began to have babies and it felt like bombs going off in my ear drums. Because the roach's legs were scratching against my ear drums, I began to scream and holler and then they came downstairs. I told them hysterically something was in my ear. They took me to the hospital and the doctor pull the roach out of my ear and told them, if they had got me there an hour later the roach would have had all its babies in my ear. I was around 10 or 11 years old and I knew this was demonic psychological abuse and it tried to destroy my life, before I became an adult.

After this, my famous brother started making a few dollars, and he decided to move far away from the house this was back in the 1980's. It was during this time we moved from the east side to the west side. This is where the mental and physical abuse continued.

CHAPTER THREE
THE MEMORIES of 20277 AVON

I was 14 years old when we moved to 20277 Avon, and this is where the abuse continued from 5830 Helen. I was a typical teenage boy. We would do what your typical teenage boys would do, such as ride bikes, go to our neighbors to play basketball, and skip school. My brother and I would do a lot of things together which included skipping school, together. With that being said, one day we decided to skip school and we went over to a cousin's house named, Aron. When we arrived to his house he ordered a pizza for us. So as a teenage boys, we continued to skip school and we continued to pastime over to our cousin's house. The first day we went, everything was cool. As I stated before, he ordered us pizza and we all ate. We sat up and talked freely, because we were comfortable being there. He was an older cousin, probably about in his early thirties, at that time. He said, if you all want to, you could come over tomorrow. So my brother said, "Okay, cool we will come over tomorrow, and we will see you, then." The second day we went over to my cousin's house and he had food ready for us to eat when we arrived. So we ate, talked, and had a lot of fun. Needless to say on the third day, we skipped school again, and returned to his house. After about 20 or 30 minutes, we looked out the door and saw a yellow and green Seville pulled into the driveway, we knew it was our brother's car. Immediately, we began to panic and we became nervous and upset. He knocked at the door and he and our mom came in and got us, and took us to the house on Avon. My mom told him to take care of us. At the age of 14, when I heard those words fear immediately struck my heart; because I knew it meant we were going to be beaten down, assaulted by my brother under the authority and sanction of my mother. Even in our mischievous actions as youth, our punishment was abuse and no one deserves to be abused, especially by a person who hands that were registered as a weapon!

When we arrived on Avon, my brother told us to go downstairs in the basement and take off all our clothes. Because of previous beat-downs, we knew to quickly obey. My brother had a dog named "Brutus". He would walk his dog with a strap about 2 inches by 5 inches. He used this really thick dog strap to whip and lash my brother and I. This particular night when he whipped us so badly, we were left bloody and bruised, to the point where actually split skin and blood was coming out of our bodies.

All of sudden, my brother's girlfriend at that time walked in and saw us laying on the floor, while we were out of it. She said we looked liked dead bodies to her, because I basically lost consciousness. When she saw us on the floor in the state we were in, she started screaming! As she screamed, I started to wake up. I don't know about my brother, whether he was conscious or not; but when she woke me up I heard her say, "What happened to them? How could y'all do them like this?" My brother the abuser said to her, "Shut up!" Then my oldest sister came and said, "It is none of your business. This is family business! You need to leave!" So she left crying.

After this beat down, my brother and I stayed out of school for about a month or so, until we healed. The wounds were so severe until our shirts would stick to our bloody bodies and the evidence of abuse would be apparently visible had we went to school. Obviously, they did not want us to go out of the house in this state. When we did returned to school I refused to get undressed and dressed for physical education class in the locker room in shame of exposing the deep slashes and whelps on my back. As a result, I failed gym class. In elementary school, I used to have counselors but I never shared the abuse that occurred in my family. As I had been trained to not reveal the abuse to outsiders. I was also told by my family that no one would believe me, anyways. I felt hopeless and unloved.

As I looked back, I feel that there should have been more done to stop the abuse and the abuser. I feel that the people who were around should have intervened. They could have made a phone call to the police or child protective services, anonymously. Maybe if they were not blinded by money, position, fame, and friendship they would not have dropped the ball and kept silent. A lot of them knew there were problems of abuse, but they refused to get involved. I never understood why my family didn't get us medical treatment. We were physically abused, mentally broken, and emotionally distraught. With the kind of abuse we suffered at the hands of our famous brother, oldest sister, and mother, it caused so much confusion for me at my young age. I needed immediate counseling! I needed much therapy! I needed help! I needed a divine intervention! I remember clearly asking, "Why? Why are the punishments so severe? Why are we being beaten until we bleed?" It was nothing I could do, but take. I had to realize as a child there was no one who would rescue me. I had to endure the pain of abuse, the beat downs from a famous brother who the whole world loved. Because, I was always told "No body is going to believe you!" I was hurt to the core of my being mentally, emotionally, and physically. Spiritually speaking, at this age I was beginning to learn about God. I remember asking God, "If you are real, why is this happening to me? Why are they beating us bloody? Do we really deserve these kind of beatings and abuse?" I was in a very dark place! The Holy Spirit said to me, "You say you are in this very dark place, and you think you have been buried. But I'm here to tell you that you are just being planted!" When the Holy Spirit told me I was being planted, and he was planting things into my life. He was beginning to heal my emotional state. He was ministering to me as I was being planted, and he was making me independent to separate me from everyone else. This is where I am today, separated. Readers, do not be afraid when you are in a dark place. Remember you are not being buried, you are just being planted. God, plants you to get you to your next level.

As an adult when I confronted my abuser about the past abusive situations, he literally told me, "It was not that bad." I was appalled when he revealed he did not think it was that bad. My life was tormented by bad memories and plagued by negative thoughts of a dysfunctional childhood. The reason why he did not think it was that bad for us is because he was not the receiving the abuse. The physical abuse caused physical wounds that healed over time. However, the abuse affected me mentally and emotionally very deeply. For any child to have to endure the abuse we endured is devastating. With that being said, after being beaten to unconsciousness I never looked at my mom the same way anymore. She allowed my famous brother the privilege to beat us. Every time an abusive incident occurred I tried to get through it and to get over it; but it was very traumatic and disheartening. Each time it happened, I relived the past over and over and I questioned my mother's love for me. I never disrespected my mom, but I stopped respecting her as a parent. I did not look at her as a parent, because I could not and I still do not understand how a parent could allow another child to beat their children bloody and not stop it. I realize early that after my father died, I had no protection and the dynamics of our family changed pertaining to me and my brother.

CHAPTER FOUR
FAMILY SEPARATION

In today's society there many types of families. A family is a group of people who are related by birth, blood, adoption, or marriage. Family can also be those you have grown up with who may not be blood related, because you all were so close, you consider them, family. An immediate family usually live under the same household with a governing authority. A good healthy family will teach, train, nurture, and discipline their children to be morally sound and refrain the ways of trouble. The relatives in the family are supposed to be loving, caring, and supportive to every person in the family. A good family will have open communication, while building an atmosphere of security and trust. Parents are supposed to reveal to their children, what their purpose is, in the earth. When parents discover and identify gifts in their children, they have a responsibility to guide their children in a positive way to develop those gifts. This will create a sense of belonging for every child in the family.

The family structure of today is a lot different from the family structure in the 1950's, 1960's and 1970's. In those days, there were no cell phones, so when a parent left the house for work he did not communicate with his family until he returned home. Families would sit down and eat dinner together at a certain time. Children went to Sunday school to learn about God. Some parents would read their children bedtime stories. Back then, we took time to build relationships with our neighbors. Our neighbors knew one another's children, because their children walked to school together and grew up together. Families were more unified even with the secrets that caused dysfunctions in the family structures.

Now in my case, our family structure consisted of the older children whipping the younger children which was very inappropriate and frankly speaking, wrong. It is not the responsibility of the older siblings to discipline the younger siblings, because they are not trained to discipline their own brothers and sister. Siblings being forced into a parental roles, and yet not knowing how to maintain a healthy relationship with the siblings they are abusively disciplining. Everything about this type of family dynamic open doors of division, separation, anger, and abuse. This is not a wholesome foundation to build a unified family structure. My older siblings abused me, they used excessive force and unconventional forms of discipline. I can truly say my older brother and sister did not know how to discipline me. The four older children were allowed to discipline the five younger children, this was not right. Legally speaking, it was not their responsibility to discipline me and my brother, but they did it anyways under the authority and permission of my mother. This caused a great separation in my family.

The undercurrent of family separation runs deep in my family. With nine siblings, and different fathers the separation in the family has been in operation a very long time. Physical abuse, psychological abuse, emotional abuse, mental abuse, and verbal abuse are all an intricate part of separating our family. It's absurd to me, for my family to abuse me and expect me to ignore the demonic acts of discipline. They want me to act like it never happened, but truth will no longer allow me to be silent. It is time for the truth to be told.

Growing up I was very adventurous, I recall a time where I was very precise in hitting a target when throwing rocks. I also was very athletic in throwing and hitting the ball. One day, Ms. Jackson the neighbor across the street, saw me hitting a tennis ball against the garage and she asked me to come and play tennis with her daughter. I started going with her to play tennis and we would have tennis matches on Saturdays. After a while, I was blessed to become so good, until no one could hit the ball when they played me. Ms. Jackson began to ask me to let them hit the ball, and get a few points. Ms. Jackson was a great supporter because, she attended all my tennis matches. She gave me the support I never received from my family. I had 20 games and none of my family members came to support me. Ms. Jackson saw athletic abilities within me and she helped me to develop greater skill in tennis. Many people at the tennis games would call me "Author Ash", liken unto the famous tennis player. Then one day I was in trouble, and my mother's way of punishing me was to not allow me to play in the championship game. Ms. Jackson begged her to allow me to go and participate, but to no avail I could not go. I cried, and Ms. Jackson cried. This altered my road of destiny, because I never picked up another tennis ball after this situation. I was psychologically and emotionally broken. Tennis was a way of escape from the dysfunctional situations in my home. My mother choice of punishment caused a greater separation in the family.

As a man now, and quite successful by God and standard of the world, the mental abuse still lingers from my family. For example, my mother refuses to acknowledge the abuse from my past. When I bring it up, she calls me crazy. When I was married and raising my children, my mother and family never celebrated me and children due to mere jealousy. I believe they truly thought I would never be anything and I would end up in a mental institution. Fortunately, here I am! I survived the abuse and made it!

Family separation is still operating in our family. A few years ago, my mother drove thirteen hours with other siblings to my city less than 5 miles from my previous home. Sadly, she visited my business briefly; but would not visit me at my own home, where there were multiple bedrooms. She and my siblings choose to stay at a relative's home where there were only 2 bedrooms. It was six adults in my mother's traveling party. It is bewildering to me how my family drove 13 hours to a city near me and would not even consider coming to visit me and my family.

In summary, it is sad when a parent cannot see great potential in all their children. Every child is unique and have different gifts, abilities, and skills. It is the responsibility of the parents to create a healthy family environment, so every child has an opportunity to explore their potential and grow with the support of their family. However, when one child is looked upon as the "golden child" and the other children, are abused, despised, and neglected it breeds an atmosphere of division and family separation that makes it difficult for total family healing. So parents if you have child who have gifts, abilities, and skills; do not neglect, abuse or belittle your other children, because you are opening spiritual doors of division and family separation.

THE HEARNS FAMILY

CHAPTER FIVE
REASONS WHY WE DON'T HAVE THE RIGHT TO REMAIN SILENT

Abuse of any kind is a sin and a criminal act of violence. It is against the law to abuse man, woman, boy, and girl whether young or old. We have a responsibility to speak up when we see, hear, or know of abuse of any kind. We <u>do not have the right to remain silent in these situations:</u>

1}. A child or adult being tied in the dark to a pole in sheets like a mummy and bound with extension cords for 24 hours .

2}. A child or adult being beat on their bear skin until they are bloody with whelps.

3}. A child being molested in their own home.

4}. A child locked in a room that has no door knobs and the windows are boarded up for days.

5}. A child forced to stand behind a door for hours with no food and water.

6}. We a friend tells you she is in an abusive relationship, and her mate is putting hands on her every chance he gets.

7}. We you see your beautician has a black eye.

8}. We your neighbor's kids comes over and you signs of physical abuse.

9}. When you see a sudden change in a child's behavior. The child was once an extrovert now is an introvert.

10}. A student requested to meet with a coach or teacher at his/her home at odd hours.

11}. Knowing a child is sick, but parents have not taken the child to the hospital to receive medical treatment.

12}. Knowing a co-worker is being sexually or racially harassed on the job, publicly.

13}. A pastor or community worker molesting children.

14}. Knowing your sibling, relative, or family members are abusing their children.

15}. Acts of incests taken place in your family.

On the previous page, we listed a few examples of abusive situations we must speak up on when we discover people connected to us are being victimized by acts of abuse. We have a responsibility not to remain silent.

As human beings, we encounter different seasons in our lives, and people have numerous reasons of why they do what they do. Really to understand the heart of an individual, you must have discernment. The gift of discerning spirits, is a gift of the Holy Spirit and it reveals the intent and motive of a person's heart. When this spiritual gift is in operation, you will know what a person intentions are, even in their silence. Silence is to remain quiet and still about something. It can be a powerful tool, because there are times when we should not speak on situations. Silence can also be detrimental when a person's life is in danger. In reiterate on the previous page, we shared incidents of abuse in which we <u>can</u> <u>not</u> <u>remain</u> <u>silent</u>.

In my family, I was trained not to talk about the dysfunctional behaviors and abuse that took place in our family and in our home. Unfortunately, I was trained psychologically to be shut my mouth and remain silent, because I was told no one would believe me. In other words, I was made to feel my voice was insignificant. I was labeled as being "crazy" and told that I was imagining things. Please know the whelps, scars, and pain of abuse is not a figment of my imagination. Name calling is a tactic the enemy uses to discredit a person who refuses to keep silent. The enemy causes a person to abuse you and then turn around and get your abuser to mock you and say all manner of evil against your falsely. His aim is to discredit the victim's mental and emotional health, so no one will believe you when you do speak the truth. It is also called, "Character Assassination". Our perpetrators want us to keep quiet about situations that would expose their demonic violations and abuse towards us. In the word of God **Ecclesiastes 3:1-8** tells us, To every thing there is a season, and a time to every purpose under the heaven: a time to be born, and a time to die; a time to plant, and a time to pluck up that which is planted; a time to kill, and a time to heal; a time to break down, and a time to build up; a time to weep, and a time to laugh; a time to mourn, and a time to dance, a time to cast away stones, and time to gather stones together; a time to embrace, and a time to refrain from embracing; a time to get, and a time to lose; a time to keep, and a time cast away; a time to rend, and a time to sew; <u>a time to keep silence, and a time to speak</u>; a time to love, and a time to hate; a time of war, and a time of peace. You can see the scriptures tell us there is a time and season for all things. There is a time to keep silence, and then there is also a time to speak.

As I stated earlier, I was abused by my famous brother, oldest sister, and my own mother all under the name of discipline. What is sad about my situation is this, there were people who were around at that time who chose to keep silent when they should have been speaking. They were more concerned about being a friend of the family, and clout chasing instead of, speaking the truth. A true friend of the family would have spoke up when they saw the unusual punishments occurring. Instead of laughing and ridiculing the me when they were told I was still standing behind the door, as usual. There is nothing normal about a child standing behind a door every time you visit. What would you have done, if you had walked in a friend's house and saw two children laying on the floor in and out of consciousness, with split skin, bloody backs, and bloody legs and begging you for help? Ask yourself, would you have kept silent like everyone else and walked out or would you have reported the obvious abuse to the proper authorities? Unfortunately, someone (KC) did walk in and did nothing? Whether it was because of fear of losing the relationship or just not wanting to get the Champ in trouble. When you choose to remain silent when people lives are in jeopardy, eventually there will be a day of judgment for you. In the Bible, the book of Galatians 6:7 says, Be not deceived; God is not mocked: for whatsoever a man soweth, that shall he also reap. Trust God, one day you will have to answered to God for being silent, when you should have spoke up. The people who were around the family when I was being abused were more concerned about keeping their jobs, getting money, and just being around the boxing world. We are living in perilous times, we are in a disturbing world where people are blinded by money, greed, and selfishness. They are only interested in what would be good for them. What would you have done if it was your child, grandchild, niece or nephew being beat until you saw blood? Would you have walked away or would you have spoke up? Are you a person who will speak up when you see ungodly abusive actions? Remember you **do not** have a right to remain silent when you see abuse!

In conclusion, silence is a sin when lives are on the line. We can not be people that claim to have love for humanity, but when we witness abuse, we wimp out and deceive ourselves into thinking we are good people. There is nothing good about abuse! We have a responsibility to hold people who we say we love, accountable for their actions when it threaten the lives of children. Lives are destroyed mentally and emotionally when the trauma of abuse is not corrected. We can not remain silent when we know abuse is taking place, because the victims of abuse lives are dispatterned and some of them are never able to fulfilled their destiny because of the psychological scars of the abuse. There are some victims of abuse who become abusers and began to repeat what has been done to them. There are others who commit suicide, because they feel their lives are worthless. Very few, are able to rise above the abuse without therapy. We must put a stop to the people who are abusers. People who abuse children show signs of neglect and they are not caring or kind to their children. Sometimes abusers repeat the abusive treatment they received as a child, or they may have been deprived while growing up. The abuser may even have low self-esteem. Some abusers think they have escaped the punishment of their abusive behaviors; because at the time they committed the abuse, everyone was too afraid to expose them. Wake up people! Don't allow their sins against you to remain silent, when you should speak up! You have a responsibility to speak up for the abuser and the victim of the abuse. You do not have the right to remain silent when someone's life is in jeopardy. At the time of my abuse, my abuser hands were registered as a lethal weapon, and yet, people who knew refused to expose the abuse, I suffered at his hands. I reiterate it is time to speak, "No more silence, and the truth shall be told, now!"

The War

PART TWO

THE PROCESS OF HEALING

I am blessed with success, in spite of my past!!!

CHAPTER SIX
THE BEGINNING OF HEALING

As we develop and mature, healing is an essential part of our ability to become whole. Being victimized by abuse, leaves a person broken, hurt, traumatized, and exasperated by feelings of negativity. There is a necessity for the victim of abuse to be healed in every aspect of his or her life: spiritually, mentally, emotionally, psychologically, and physically. Healing means to become healthy and sound again. It means to make better and to make well again by moving through the pain of trauma and any situation trying to detour one from walking in their true purpose. It gives the connotation of one being strengthen to endure life encounters again. This means you must forgive your abuser, forgive yourself, and forgive others who knew your situation; but refuse to speak up, intervene and help.

To begin the healing process of childhood abuse, the victim has to detach and get away from his or her abuser. As a victim of abuse, I have learned to distance myself from my abusers and the toxic people connected to all the situations of the abuse. I discovered it is important for me to stay out of the atmosphere and events where my abusers may frequent; to prevent my thinking from being drawn back to the past. I realized for me it is not healthy to be near them, because seeing them ignites the triggers of trauma and bad memories of my past. Secondly, being a victim of abuse means you must stop communicating with your abusers, because every time you communicate with them the enemy may use your abuser to entice you to go back to your past. If you are not careful it can pull you into a cycle of negative thoughts, and negative emotions. Next, you have to build a personal relationship with God, so you can pray for your own healing. Believing in God, exercising faith, and praying is the foundation necessary for you to heal your heart and mind, spiritually and mentally. Our relationship with God is crucial to building our faith and giving us the confidence of knowing that our prayers will be answered. Remember prayer turns pain into power!

Fourth, in the process of healing it is imperative to reduce and eliminate stress. You have to participate in activities that ensure your own personal happiness. Engage in activities that make you happy; such as, exercising, fishing, sporting events, spend time at the park, writing, bowling, reading a book, take a vacation, meditate, rest and relaxation, meeting new friends, open a business, skating, or shopping. You can have a spa day, get a make over, or do what ever makes you happy. You must learn to love yourself, trust yourself and spoil yourself. When a person has been abused there is a lot that has been taken from you. An intricate part of being restored in your healing is, you have to learn how to put everything back into you that was taken out of you. When the healing process is in operation you will begin to enjoy your life. You must indulge in the goodness of life this will begin to truly heal you. Remember to stay focused and pray, pray, pray, and pray!

CHAPTER SEVEN
OVERCOMING THE ANGER

The anger, hurt, and disappointment incurred while being victimized by child abuse runs deep within the heart of any victim. Sometimes people who have experienced childhood trauma like myself, are tormented by bad memories of the abuse, deep hurt, distrust in relationships, and constant anger. Anger is defined as a strong sense of displeasure, annoyance, indignation, vexation, infuriation, outraged, rage, and madness. A person with anger can be passive aggressive or aggressive aggressive in their display of anger. Passive aggressive anger causes a person to be silent in their anger. This person will be resistant to the requests, instructions, or demands of others. They will sometimes refuse communication and avoid confrontations with the person who have wronged them. Aggressive aggressive anger causes a person to become destructive and violent in their anger. Which often times involve physical harm, destroying property, and self-harming behaviors. When a child has experienced abuse, anger becomes a survival emotion to respond to the trauma that destroyed their child development.

For me anger helped me to cope with the abuse. I did not understand how someone who suppose to love you could abused you and then live everyday life like nothing ever happened. As a child, I was forced to be silent, and made to act like my abusers, as if nothing was happening to me. All the trauma I experienced caused me to question God. I asked Him, "Why me? What do I have to go through all of this? Why is this happening to me?" I was devastated! The hardest part of everything is, they refused to apologize for all of the abuse they did to me. They would not own up to what happen during my childhood and they would not acknowledge the wrong they did to me. I was overwhelmed by the severe injustice that I encountered from my family members. This trauma tried to ruin and destroy my life. They continue to say I'm crazy, and it's just in my head. The mental and physical scars are not a figment of my imagination. The abuse was real; and the pain and bad memories was put in my head because they brutally and repeatedly used me as an escape goat and punching bag. I was frustrated, angry, and silenced!

I vowed not to be an abusive man. I decided would not abuse the people I love. I refused to allow the trauma of abuse to cycle me in the same mentally as my family members, the abusers. Of course, they want me to forget about it, and they want me to make it seem like nothing happened. That is difficult for me to do because I have not received an official apology. Everyone refuse to own up to their part of the ill treatment, psychological and physical abuse. I guess in their world, what they did to me was alright. I remember asking my brother why did he do the things he did to me and his response was, "It wasn't that bad." How can abuse not be bad? No it was not bad to him, because he didn't experienced it. He was the one doing the abuse to me. He was not receiving it. So that is why he thought it wan't that bad!

I know for a fact, some people who have experienced the childhood trauma of abuse do not make it to the point where I am in life, today. Many would have committed suicide by now or been mentally institutionalized. I tried several times to attempt suicide, at least five times. However, every time I tried it would not work. It was like God had his arms around me every time. He said, "I have every bit of your life in my hands, and I have purpose for you!" Because every time I tried to commit suicide, they would find me and take me to the hospital. I remember taking pills several times, and even jumping out of a window trying to escape the pain, shame, and anger of abuse. My family would tell the doctors, "He's crazy." I did not receive any therapy, because they did not want to risk me revealing how I was being abused at home.

In summary reader, if you have been abused as a child, you have to overcome your anger and pick yourself so you can live your own life. Through my relationship with God, I am able to live life through his healing virtue. He taught me how to release the anger, walk in forgiveness and speak my truth! No more silence!

CHAPTER EIGHT
UNDERSTANDING MY PURPOSE

Do you know your purpose? Everyone was born with a purpose. It is important for us to discover our purpose. Our parents should guide and assist us in our process of discovering our purpose. Sometimes parents neglect to see who their children are and why God created them. This means some children are left confused and misguided about who they are and what they were born to accomplish in life. Purpose entails the reason why you were created. It deals with the reason why something or someone exists. Your purpose is God's plan for your life. It is sad that some people never really understand or achieve their purpose, Some people are detoured, derailed, and dis-patterned from the purpose and destiny God have for their lives, due to the abuse and trauma in their childhood.. Unfortunately, some people also miss their purpose, because of generational curses which interfere with their abilities to develop into the person God wants them to be. I have seen people paralyzed by childhood abuse and they are tormented by the horrific memories of their past. They are oppressed mentally, internally frustrated, filled with bitterness of soul, and emotionally cold until they become out of touch with the reality of life. This is the assignment of satan to stop a person before they are able to understand their purpose. Childhood abuse can destroy a person's mind and hinder them from fulfilling purpose. I am grateful and thankful to God, that in spite of the abuse and trauma I experienced as a child, I was still able to discover and understand my purpose in this world.

We had a family Chef, named Sam Fenton, who was instrumental in me discovering my niche of cooking. I used to always confide in him, and his trust caused me to believe in him, because he would always listen to me. Chef Fenton understood and knew I was being falsely accused, and blamed for things I did not do. He would see and address it. He was fired because he was told he was getting too much in the family business. Chef Fenton tried to take me from my family, and he inspired me to become a chef. He encouraged me to pursue my own career, and branch off from the family.

My career began at 16 years old when I worked several jobs in the food industry. I have worked in many restaurants as a chef. My career increased and soared upon moving to Memphis, Tennessee. I took northern style of cooking and turned it into the southern hit! I have owned restaurants and clubs in Michigan and Mississippi. I have also been the private chef for the late Bishop G.E. Patterson, Presiding Bishop of Church of God in Christ, two years before his passing. I have cooked for their Holy Convocation General Board for the Church of God in Christ. God has been faithful to me, as I operated in my purpose of cooking. From fine dining, family restaurants, food trucks, creating my own seasonings, to growing healthy vegetable gardens. I have been extremely successful in my profession, in spite of all the abuse and trauma I experienced growing up.

I realize in writing this book, an intricate part of my purpose is to help others to be heal, especially those who have experienced the same thing I have been through. I want them to know they do not have to remain silent about their childhood trauma all their life. There is a point and time where you must release and tell your story. You can not remain silent because the silence will eat you up on the inside, and it will mentally destroy you. You must discover your purpose by realizing that the childhood abuse does not dictate your future. In spite of the terrible abuse that happened in your childhood, you still can be healed from the abuse and help others to be healed too! Don't allow the abuse to destroy you spiritually, mentally, emotionally, nor physically. Let go, open your mouth, come out with your story! It's time for you to speak your truth! No more silence!

No More Silence &
The Truth Shall Be Told

CHEF JESSIE B. HEARNS
On my way to cook for over 5,000 People for the COGIC Convocation!

The late Bishop G. E. Patterson

Jessie B's Restaurants
in Patel & Hattiesburg, Mississippi

CHAPTER NINE
NO MORE SILENCE

Have you ever experienced something so devastating in your childhood until you vowed to yourself that you would take it to your grave? Well, the enemy wants to destroy you! He wants to destroy your purpose before you began to walk on your road of destiny. He comes to steal, kill, and destroy your life. It is through the power of God, you can enjoy life and have it in abundance. You do not have to remain silent, anymore. Whatever horrifying event you experienced in your childhood, happened to stop your progression. It wants you to be stifled in your development of purpose. You can no longer allow bad memories and childhood trauma to control your life. The trauma wants to subconsciously direct your decisions in life. It wants to create cycles of distrust, insecurities, and failure. When a person has unresolved hurt and no closure from past trauma, it is difficult to build new personal relationships. Being silent when you have been hurt, rejected, or abused; can destroy you mentally, physically, and psychologically and if you are not careful, spiritually. The reason why I say spiritually, is because you will begin to question God, "Why me? Lord, why would you allow this to happen to me?" It causes you to ask God, "Why is it taking so long for justice to be served on my behalf?" As a young child, you don't understand that God does things in His own timing. The word of God says, "Dearly beloved, avenge not yourselves, but rather give place unto wrath: for it is written, Vengeance is mine; I will repay, saith the Lord," according to Romans 12:19. The undercurrent of broken dreams, betrayal, and disappointment can weigh heavy on the heart and mind of a victim. It is important for you to speak out early, because the earlier you open up and speak up the better you will be. Don't be afraid to dial 911 yourself. The enemy will try to bring thoughts of shame and guilt; but you must be determined to speak up. The enemy wants you to be hurt and broken on the inside, so can not achieve success in a healthy manner. He wants to silence you through childhood abuse and trauma. You can not allow him to intimidate you through the opinions of others. There will be people who are angry with you for speaking your truth and there will people who agree with you for exposing the person who wronged you. No matter what people think, say, or believe you must speak your truth. It is time for you to open your mouth, release the trauma, and expose the abuser. This is your time for "No More Silence!"

Jessie B's started his business at a car wash in Memphis, Tennessee on the corner of Ridgeway and Mt. Moriah.

Jessie B
Became famous for his cooking skills!

WHOEVER COUNTED ME OUT,

COULDN'T COUNT!

COMING SOON!

www.ingramcontent.com/pod-product-compliance
Lightning Source LLC
Chambersburg PA
CBHW070337230426
43663CB00011B/2362